Promises

Poems 1954-1956

Books by Robert Penn Warren

John Brown: The Making of a Martyr
Thirty-Six Poems
Eleven Poems on the Same Theme
Night Rider
Selected Poems, 1923–1943
At Heaven's Gate
All the King's Men
The Circus in the Attic
World Enough and Time
Brother to Dragons
Band of Angels
Segregation: The Inner Conflict in the South
Promises: Poems 1954–1956

Robert Penn Warren

Promises

Poems 1954-1956

Random House, New York

To Rosanna and Gabriel

Contents

To a Little Girl, One Year Old, in a Ruined Fortress

To Rosanna

I Sirocco

To a place of ruined stone we brought you, and sea-reaches.
Rocca: fortress, hawk-heel, lion-paw, clamped on a hill.
A hill, no. Sea cliff, and crag-cocked, the embrasures commanding the beaches,
Range easy, with most fastidious mathematic and skill.

Philipus me fecit: he of Spain, the black-browed, the anguished,
For whom nothing prospered, though he loved God.
His arms, great scutcheon of stone, once at drawbridge, have now languished
Long in the moat, under garbage; at moat-brink, rosemary with blue,
                                        thistle with gold bloom, nod.

Sun blaze and cloud tatter, it is the sirocco, the dust swirl is swirled
Over the bay face, mounts air like gold gauze whirled; it traverses
                                        the blaze-blue of water.
We have brought you where geometry of a military rigor survives
                                        its own ruined world,
And sun regilds your gilt hair, in the midst of your laughter.

Rosemary, thistle, clutch stone. Far hangs Giannutri in blue air. Far to that blueness
                                        the heart aches,
And on the exposed approaches the last gold of gorse bloom, in the sirocco, shakes.

3

II Gull's Cry

White goose by palm tree, palm ragged, among stones the white oleander,
And the she-goat, brown, under pink oleander, waits.
I do not think that anything in the world will move, not goat, not gander.
Goat droppings are fresh in the hot dust; not yet the beetle; the sun beats,

And under blue shadow of mountain, over blue-braiding sea-shadow,
The gull hangs white; whiter than white against mountain-mass,
The gull extends motionless on shelf of air, on substance of shadow.
The gull, at an eye-blink, will, into the astonishing statement of sun, pass.

All night, next door, the defective child cried; now squats in the dust
            where the lizard goes.
The wife of the *gobbo* sits under vine leaves, she suffers, her eyes glare.
The engaged ones sit in the privacy of bemusement, heads bent: the classic pose.
Let the beetle work, the gull comment the irrelevant anguish of air,

But at your laughter let the molecular dance of the stone-dark
        glimmer like joy in the stone's dream,
And in that moment of possibility, let *gobbo, gobbo's* wife, and us, and all,
        take hands and sing: redeem, redeem!

4

I I I The Child Next Door

The child next door is defective because the mother,
Seven brats already in that purlieu of dirt,
Took a pill, or did something to herself she thought would not **hurt**,
But it did, and no good, for there came this monstrous other.

The sister is twelve. Is beautiful like a saint.
Sits with the monster all day, with pure love, calm eyes.
Has taught it a trick, to make *ciao*, Italian-wise.
It crooks hand in that greeting. She smiles her smile without taint.

I come, and her triptych beauty and joy stir hate
—Is it hate?—in my heart. Fool, doesn't she know that the process
Is not that joyous or simple, to bless, or unbless,
The malfeasance of nature or the filth of fate?

Can it bind or loose, that beauty in that kind,
Beauty of benediction? I trust our hope to prevail
That heart-joy in beauty be wisdom, before beauty fail
And be gathered like air in the ruck of the world's wind!

I think of your goldness, of joy, how empires grind, stars are hurled.
I smile stiff, saying *ciao*, saying *ciao*, and think: this is the world.

5

I V   The Flower

Above the beach, the vineyard
Terrace breaks to the seaward
Drop, where the cliffs fail
To a clutter of manganese shale.
Some is purple, some powdery-pale.
But the black lava-chunks stand off
The sea's grind, or indolent chuff.
The lava will withstand
The sea's beat, or insinuant hand,
And protect our patch of sand.

It is late. The path from the beach
Crawls up. I take you. We reach
The vineyard, and at that path angle
The hedge obtrudes a tangle
Of leaf and green bulge and a wrangle
Bee-drowsy and blowsy with white bloom,
Scarcely giving the passer-by room.
We know that that blossomy mass
Will brush our heads as we pass,

6

And at knee there's gold gorse and blue clover,
And at ankle, blue *malva* all over
—Plus plants I don't recognize
With my non-botanical eyes.
We approach, but before we get there,
If no breeze stirs that green lair,
The scent and sun-honey of air
Is too sweet comfortably to bear.

I carry you up the hill.
In my arms you are sweet and still.
We approach your special place,
And I am watching your face
To see the sweet puzzlement grow,
And then recognition glow.
Recognition explodes in delight.
You leap like spray, or like light.
Despite my arm's tightness,
You leap in gold-glitter and brightness.
You leap like a fish-flash in bright air,
And reach out. Yes, I'm well aware
That this is the spot, and hour,
For you to demand your flower.

When first we came this way
Up from the beach, that day
That seems now so long ago,
We moved bemused and slow
In the season's pulse and flow.
Bemused with sea, and slow
With June heat and perfume,
We paused here, and plucked you a bloom.
So here you always demand
Your flower to hold in your hand,
And the flower must be white,

7

For you have your own ways to compel
Observance of this ritual.
You hold it and sing with delight.
And your mother, for our own delight,
Picks one of the blue flowers there,
To put in your yellow hair.
That done, we go on our way
Up the hill, toward the end of the day.

But the season has thinned out.
From the bay edge below, the shout
Of a late bather reaches our ear,
Coming to the vineyard here
By more than distance thinned.
The bay is in shadow, the wind
Nags the shore to white.
The mountain prepares the night.
By the vineyard we have found
No bloom worthily white,
And the few we have found
Not disintegrated to the ground
Are by season and sea-salt browned.
We give the best one to you.
It is ruined, but will have to do.
Somewhat better the blue blossoms fare.
We find one for your hair,
And you sing as though human need
Were not for perfection. We proceed
Past floss-borne or sloughed-off seed,
Past curled leaf and dry pod,
And the blue blossom will nod
With your head's drowsy gold nod.

Let all seasons pace their power,
As this has paced to this hour.

Let season and season devise
Their possibilities.
Let the future reassess
All past joy, and past distress,
Till we know Time's deep intent,
And the last integument
Of the past shall be rent
To show how all things bent
Their energies to that hour
When you first demanded your flower.

And in that image let
Both past and future forget,
In clasped communal ease,
Their brute identities.

The path lifts up ahead
To the *rocca*, supper, bed.
We move in the mountain's shade.
But the mountain is at our back.
Ahead, climbs the coast-cliff track.
The valley between is dim.
Ahead, on the cliff rim,
The *rocca* clasps its height.
It accepts the incipient night.
Just once we look back.
On sunset, a white gull is black.
It hangs over the mountain crest.
It hangs on that saffron west.
It makes its outcry.
It slides down the sky.
East now, it catches the light.
Its black has gone again white,
And over the *rocca's* height
It gleams in the last light.

9

It has sunk from our sight.
Beyond the cliff is night.

It sank on unruffled wing.
We hear the sea rustling.

It will rustle all night, darling.

V Colder Fire

It rained toward day. The morning came sad and white
With silver of sea-sadness and defection of season.
Our joys and convictions are sure, but in that wan light
We moved—your mother and I—in muteness of spirit past logical reason.

Now sun, afternoon, and again summer-glitter on sea.
As you to a bright toy, the heart leaps. The heart unlocks
Joy, though we know, shamefaced, the heart's weather should not be
Merely a reflex to solstice, or sport of some aggrieved equinox.

No, the heart should be steadfast: I know that.
And I sit in the late-sunny lee of the watch-house,
At the fortress point, you on my knee now, and the late
White butterflies over gold thistle conduct their ritual carouse.

In whisperless carnival, in vehemence of gossamer,
Pale ghosts of pale passions of air, the white wings weave.
In tingle and tangle of arabesque, they mount light, pair by pair,
As though that tall light were eternal indeed, not merely the summer's reprieve.

11

You leap on my knee, you exclaim at the sun-stung gyration.
And the upper air stirs, as though the vast stillness of sky
Had stirred in its sunlit sleep and made a suspiration,
A luxurious languor of breath, as after love, there is a sigh.

But enough, for the highest sun-scintillant pair are gone
Seaward, past rampart and cliff borne, over blue sea-gleam.
Close to my chair, to a thistle, a butterfly sinks now, flight done.
By gold bloom of thistle, white wings pulse under the sky's dream.

The sky's dream is enormous, I lift up my eyes.
In sunlight a tatter of mist clings high on the mountain-mass.
The mountain is under the sky, and there the gray scarps rise
Past paths where on their appointed occasions men climb, and pass.

Past grain-patch, last apron of vineyard, last terrace of olive,
Past chestnut, past cork grove, where the last carts can go,
Past camp of the charcoal maker, where coals glow in the black hive,
The scarps, gray, rise up. Above them is that place I know.

The pines are there, they are large, a deep recess,
Shelf above scarp, enclave of rock, a glade
Benched and withdrawn in the mountain-mass, under the peak's duress.
We came there—your mother and I—and rested in that severe shade.

Pine-blackness mist-tangled, the peak black above: the glade gives
On the empty threshold of air, the hawk-hung delight
Of distance unspooled and bright space spilled—ah, the heart thrives!
We stood in that shade and saw sea and land lift in the far light.

Now the butterflies dance, time-tattered and disarrayed.
I watch them. I think how above that far scarp's sunlit wall
Mist threads in silence the darkness of boughs, and in that shade
Condensed moisture gathers at needle-tip. It glitters, will fall.

I cannot interpret for you this collocation
Of memories. You will live your own life, and contrive

The language of your own heart, but let that conversation,
In the last analysis, be always of whatever truth you would live.

For fire flames but in the heart of a colder fire.
All voice is but echo caught from a soundless voice.
Height is not deprivation of valley, nor defect of desire,
But defines, for the fortunate, that joy in which all joys should rejoice.

13

Promises

To Gabriel

I What Was the Promise That Smiled
                                    from the Maples at Evening?

What was the promise that smiled from the maples at evening?
Smiling dim from the shadow, recessed? What language of leaf-lip?
And the heels of the fathers clicked on the concrete, returning,
Each aware of his own unspecified burden, at sun-dip.
Beneath pale hydrangeas first firefly utters cold burning.
The sun is well down now, first star has now winked.

What was the promise when bullbats dizzied the sunset?
They skimmer and skitter in gold light at great height.
The guns of big boys on the common go *boom*, past regret.
Boys shout when hit bullbat spins down in that gold light.
"Too little to shoot"—but next year you'll be a big boy.
So shout now and pick up the bird—Why, that's blood, it is wet.
Its eyes are still open, your heart in the throat swells like joy.

What was the promise when, after the last light had died,
Children gravely, down walks, in spring dark, under maples, drew
Trains of shoe boxes, empty, with windows, with candles inside,
Going *chuck-chuck*, and blowing for crossings, lonely, *oo-oo*?
But on impulse you fled, and they called, called across the dark lawn,

17

Long calling your name, who now lay in the darkness to hide,
While the sad little trains glimmer on under maples, and on.

What was the promise when, after the dying was done,
All the long years before, like burnt paper, flared into black,
And the house shrunk to silence, the odor of flowers near gone?
Recollection of childhood was natural: cold gust at the back.
What door on the dark flings open, then suddenly bangs?
Yes, something was lost in between, but it's long, the way back.
You sleep, but in sleep hear a door that creaks where it hangs.

Long since, in a cold and coagulate evening, I've stood
Where they slept, the long dead, and the farms and far woods fled away,
And a gray light prevailed and both landscape and heart were subdued.
Then sudden, the ground at my feet was like glass, and I say
What I saw, saw deep down, and the fleshly habiliments rent—
But agleam in a phosphorus of glory, bones bathed, there they lay,
Side by side, Ruth and Robert: the illumination then spent.

Earth was earth, and in earth-dark no glow now, therefore I lifted
My gaze to that world which had once been the heart's familiar,
Swell of woods and far field-sweep, in twilight by stream-gleam now wefted,
Railroad yonder and coal chute, town roofs far under the first star.
Then her voice, long forgotten, calm in silence, said: "Child."
Then his, with the calm of a night field, or far star:
"We died only that every promise might be fulfilled."

r

II Court-martial

Under the cedar tree,
He would sit, all summer, with me:
An old man and small grandson
Withdrawn from the heat of the sun.

Captain, cavalry, C.S.A.,
An old man, now shrunken, gray,
Pointed beard clipped the classic way,
Tendons long gone crank and wry,
And long shrunken the cavalryman's thigh
Under the pale-washed blue jean.
His pipe smoke lifts, serene
Beneath boughs of the evergreen,
With sunlight dappling between.
I see him now, as once seen.

Light throbs the far hill.
The boughs of the cedar are still.

His years like landscape lie
Spread to the backward eye

In life's long irony.
All the old hoofbeats fade
In the calm of the cedar shade,
Where only the murmur and hum
Of the far farm, and summer, now come.
He can forget all—forget
Even mortgage and lien and debt,
Cutworm and hail and drouth,
Bang's disease, hoof-and-mouth,
Barn sagging and broken house—
For now in the shade, adrowse,
At last he can sit, or rouse
To light pipe, or say to me
Some scrap of old poetry—
Byron or Burns—and idly
The words glimmer and fade
Like sparks in the dark of his head.

In the dust by his chair
I undertook to repair
The mistakes of his old war.
Hunched on that toy terrain,
Campaign by campaign,
I sought, somehow, to untie
The knot of History,
For in our shade I knew
That only the Truth is true,
That life is only the act
To transfigure all fact,
And life is only a story
And death is only the glory
Of the telling of the story,
And the *done* and the *to-be-done*
In that timelessness were one,
Beyond the poor *being done*.

20

The afternoon stood still.
Sun dazzled the far hill.

It was only a chance word
That a chance recollection had stirred.
"Guerrilla—what's that?" I said.
"Bushwhackers, we called 'em," he said.
"Were they on the Yankee side?"
"Son, they didn't have any side.
Just out to plunder and ride
And hell-rake the pore countryside.
Just out for themselves, so, son,
If you happened to run across one,
Or better, laid hand to a passel,
No need to be squeamish, or wrestle
Too long with your conscience. But if—"
He paused, raised his pipe, took a whiff—
"If your stomach or conscience was queasy,
You could make it all regular, easy.

"By the road, find some shade, a nice patch.
Even hackberry does, at a scratch.
Find a spring with some cress fresh beside it,
Growing rank enough to nigh hide it.
Lord, a man can sure thirst when you ride.
Yes, find you a nice spot to bide.
Bide sweet when you can when you ride.
Order halt, let heat-daze subside.
Put your pickets, vedettes out, dismount.
Water horses, grease gall, take count,
And while the men rest and jaw,
You and two lieutenants talk law.
Brevitatem justitia amat.
Time is short—hell, a rope is—that's that."

21

That was that, and the old eyes were closed.
On a knee one old hand reposed,
Fingers crooked on the cob pipe, where
Last smoke raveled blue up the air.
Every tale has an end, has an end.
But smoke rose, did not waver or bend.
It unspooled, wouldn't stop, wouldn't end.

"By God—" and he jerked up his head.
"By God, they deserved it," he said.
"Don't look at me that way," he said.
"By God—" and the old eyes glared red.
Then shut in the cedar shade.

The head slept in that dusk the boughs made.
The world's silence made me afraid.
Then a July-fly, somewhere,
Like silk ripping, ripped the bright air.
Then stopped. Sweat broke in my hair.

I snatched my gaze away.
I swung to the blazing day.
Ruined lawn, raw house swam in light.
The far woods swam in my sight.
Throbbing, the fields fell away
Under the blaze of day.

Calmly then, out of the sky,
Blotting the sun's blazing eye,
He rode. He was large in the sky.
Behind, shadow massed, slow, and grew
Like cloud on the sky's summer blue.
Out of that shade-mass he drew.
To the great saddle's sway, he swung,
Not old now, not old now, but young,
Great cavalry boots to the thigh,

No speculation in eye.
Then clotting behind him, and dim,
Clot by clot, from the shadow behind him,
They took shape, enormous in air.
Behind him, enormous, they hung there:

Ornaments of the old rope,
Each face outraged, agape,
Not yet believing it true.
Each hairy jaw is askew,
Tongue out, out-staring eye,
And the spittle not yet dry
That was uttered with the last cry.

The horseman does not look back.
Blank-eyed, he continues his track,
Riding toward me there,
Through the darkening air.

The world is real. It is there.

III   Gold Glade

Wandering, in autumn, the woods of boyhood,
Where cedar, black, thick, rode the ridge,
Heart aimless as rifle, boy-blankness of mood,
I came where ridge broke, and the great ledge,
Limestone, set the toe high as treetop by dark edge

Of a gorge, and water hid, grudging and grumbling,
And I saw, in mind's eye, foam white on
Wet stone, stone wet-black, white water tumbling,
And so went down, and with some fright on
Slick boulders, crossed over. The gorge-depth drew night on,

But high over high rock and leaf-lacing, sky
Showed yet bright, and declivity wooed
My foot by the quietening stream, and so I
Went on, in quiet, through the beech wood:
There, in gold light, where the glade gave, it stood.

The glade was geometric, circular, gold,
No brush or weed breaking that bright gold of leaf-fall.

24

In the center it stood, absolute and bold
Beyond any heart-hurt, or eye's grief-fall.
Gold-massy in air, it stood in gold light-fall,

No breathing of air, no leaf now gold-falling,
No tooth-stitch of squirrel, or any far fox bark,
No woodpecker coding, or late jay calling.
Silence: gray-shagged, the great shagbark
Gave forth gold light. There could be no dark.

But of course dark came, and I can't recall
What county it was, for the life of me.
Montgomery, Todd, Christian—I know them all.
Was it even Kentucky or Tennessee?
Perhaps just an image that keeps haunting me.

No, no! in no mansion under earth,
Nor imagination's domain of bright air,
But solid in soil that gave it its birth,
It stands, wherever it is, but somewhere.
I shall set my foot, and go there.

I V Dark Woods

1 *Tonight the Woods Are Darkened*

Tonight the woods are darkened.
  You have, long back, forgot
What impulse or perturbation
  Had made you rise. You went out

Of the house, where faces and light were,
  To walk, and the night was black.
The dog whined. He tried to follow.
  You picked up some rocks. Rocked him back.

One yelp the brute gave from back there.
  Good. So now you were free
To enter the field and dark there
  Under your heart's necessity.

Under sparse star-gleam a glimmer
  Of pale dust provoked your feet
To pursue the ectoplasmic bisection
  Of the dark field-heave, and to meet,

Yonder where woods massed their darkness,
  A darkness more absolute.
All right: and in shadow the pale dust,
  How soundless, accepted the foot!

Foot trapped in that silken compulsion
  Of dust, and dust-softness, and the pale
Path's glimmer in field-darkness,
  You moved. Did nerve fail?

Could you stop? No, all's re-enactment.
  Trapped in that *déjà-vu,*
Déjà-fait, déjà-fait, you hear whispers,
  In the dark, say, "Ah." Say: "You, too?"

Was there a field full of folk there,
  Behind you? Threading like mist?
All who, dark-hungry, once had flung forth
  From the house, and now persist

In the field-dark to spy on and count you—
  They who now rejoice not, nor grieve,
But yet leer in their spooky connivance,
  Waiting to pluck sleeve?

You wheel now to face them, but nothing
  Is there. Only you. And in starlight,
Beyond the old field and pale cow-track,
  The woods wait. They wait. *All right.*

27

2   The Dogwood

All right: and with that wry acceptance you follow the cow-track.
Yes, it's dark in the woods, as black as a peddler's pocket.
Cobweb tangles, briar snatches. A sensible man would go back.
A bough finds your face, and one eye grieves in the socket.

Midnight compounds with the peeper. Now whippoorwills speak,
Far off. Then silence. What's that? And something blots star—
By your head velvet air-*whoosh,* curdle and shudder of wing-creak.
It is only an owl. You go on. You can guess where you are.

For here is the gum-swamp, the slough where you once trapped the weasel.
Here the dead cow was dumped, and by buzzards duly divested.
All taint of mortality's long since wiped clean as a whistle.
Now love vine threads eyehole, God's peace is by violet attested.

The bones are long lost. In green grass the skull waits, has waited:
A cathedral for ants, and at noon, under white dome, great transept,
They pass in green gloom, under sunlight by leaf mitigated,
For leaf of the love vine shuts eyehole, as though the eye slept.

28

But now it's not noon, it is night, and ant-dark in that cow skull.
And man-dark in the woods. But go on, that's how men survive.
Went on in the dark, heart tight now as nut in the hull.
Came back in the dark, and home, and throve as men thrive.

But not before you had seen it, sudden at path-turn,
White-floating in darkness, the dogwood, white bloom in dark air.
Like an ice-break, broke joy; then you felt a strange wrath burn
To strike it, and strike, had a stick been handy in the dark there.

But one wasn't handy, so there on the path now, breath scant,
You stood, you stood there, and oh, could the poor heart's absurd
Cry for wisdom, for wisdom, ever be answered? Triumphant,
All night, the tree glimmered in darkness, and uttered no word.

3 The Hazel Leaf

Tonight the woods are darkened.
   You have forgotten what pain
Had once drawn you forth:
    To remember it might yet be some pain.
    But to forget may, too, be pain.

The hazel leaf falls in autumn.
   It slants athwart the gold air.
Boys come, prompt at nut-fall,
    To shout and kick up the gold leaves there.
    Shouts echo in high boughs not yet bare.

The hazel leaf falls in autumn.
   Boys go, and no voices intrude
Now at dusk-hour. The foot
    Of only the squirrel stirs leaf of this solitude.
    Otherwise, only shadow may now intrude.

The little green snake by the path-side,
   In May, lifts its jeweled head.

It stares, waves the tongue-wisp.
   What it hears on the path is not now your tread.
   But it still stares with lifted head.

Yes, your tread's now fainter and farther.
   Years muffle a tread, like grass.
Who passed, struck; now goes on.
   The snake waits, head crushed, to be observed by the next to pass.
   He will observe it, and then pass.

Tonight the woods are darkened.
   What other man may go there
Now stares, silent, breath scant,
   Waiting for the white petal to be released in dark air.
   Do not forget you were once there.

V   Country Burying (1919)

A thousand times you've seen that scene:
  Oak grove, bare ground, little white church there,
Bone-white in that light, and through dust-pale green
  Of oak leaf, the steeple pokes up in the bright air.

For it is summer, and once I sat
  At grove-edge beyond the disarray
Of cars in the shade-patch, this way and that.
  They stood patient as mules now in the heat of the day.

Chevrolet, T-Model, a Hudson or two,
  They are waiting like me, and the afternoon glares.
Waiting is all they have come to do.
  What goes on inside is no concern of theirs,

Nor of mine, who have lost a boy's afternoon,
  When summer's so short, oh, so short, just to bring
My mother to bury someone she'd scarce known.
  "I respect her," she'd said, but was that enough of a thing?

Who was she? Who knows? I'd not thought to ask it.
    That kind came to town, in buggy or Ford,
Some butter to swap, clutch of eggs in a basket,
    Gnarled hands in black mittens, old face yellow as a gourd.

It's no matter now who lies in the church,
    Where heads bend in duty in sparse rows.
Green miles of tobacco, sun-dazzled, stretch
    Away. Red clay, the road winds, goes on where it goes.

And we, too, now go, down the road, where it goes,
    My mother and I, the hole now filled.
Light levels in fields now, dusk crouches in hedgerows,
    As we pass from what is, toward what will be, fulfilled,

And I passed toward voices and the foreign faces,
    Knew dawn in strange rooms, and the heart gropes for center,
But should I come back, and come back where that place is,
    Oak grove, white church, in day-glare a-daze, I might enter.

For what? But enter, and find what I'd guess:
    The odor of varnish, hymnals stacked on a chair,
Light religiously dim by painted paper on window glass,
    And the insistent buzz of a fly lost in shadow, somewhere.

Why doesn't that fly stop buzzing—stop buzzing up there!

33

VI School Lesson Based on Word of Tragic Death
of Entire Gillum Family

They weren't so bright, or clean, or clever,
　　And their noses were sometimes imperfectly blown,
But they always got to school the weather whatever,
　　With old lard pail full of fried pie, smoked ham, and corn pone.

It was good six miles to the Gillum place,
　　Back where the cedar and hoot owl consorted
And the snapping turtle snoozed in his carapace
　　And the whang-doodle whooped and the dang-whoodle snorted.

Tow hair was thick as a corn-shuck mat.
　　They had milky blue eyes in matching pairs.
And barefoot or brogan, when they sat,
　　Their toes were the kind that hook round the legs of chairs.

They had adenoids to make you choke,
　　And buttermilk breath, and their flannels asteam,
And sat right mannerly while teacher spoke,
　　But when book-time came their eyes were glazed and adream.

34

There was Dollie-May, Susie-May, Forrest, Sam, Brother—
    Thirteen down to eight the stairsteps ran.
They had popped right natural from their big fat mother,
    The clabber kind that can catch just by honing after a man.

She must have honed hard, and maybe had to,
    For Old Slat Gillum was the kind of a one
Who wasn't designed to cast much shadow
    If set a little sideways and not in good strong sun.

But she had her brood, and that was that,
    Though you wondered how she had relished her reaming,
For from yellow toenail to old black felt hat,
    Gillum was scarcely the type to set a lady dreaming.

In town he'd stop, and say: "Say, mister,
    I'll name you what's true fer folks, ever-one.
Human-man ain't much more'n a big blood blister,
    All red and proud-swole, but one good squeeze and he's gone.

"Take me, ain't wuth lead and powder to perish,
    Just some spindle bone stuck in a pair of pants,
But a man's got his chaps to love and to cherish,
    And raise up and larn 'em so they kin git they chance."

So mud to the hub, or dust to the hock,
    God his helper, wet or dry,
Old Gillum swore by God and by cock,
    He'd git 'em larned before his own time came to die.

That morning blew up cold and wet,
    All the red-clay road was curdled as curd,
And no Gillums there for the first time yet.
    The morning drones on. Stove spits. Recess. Then the word.

Dollie-May was combing Susie-May's head.
    Sam was feeding, Forrest milking, got nigh through.

Little Brother just sat on the edge of his bed.
    Somebody must have said: "Pappy, what now you aimin' to do?"

An ice pick is a subtle thing.
    The puncture's small, blood only a wisp.
It hurts no more than a bad bee sting.
    When the sheriff got there the school-bread was long burned to a crisp.

In the afternoon silence the chalk would scrape.
    We sat and watched the windowpanes steam,
Blur the old corn field and accustomed landscape.
    Voices came now faint in our intellectual dream.

Which shoe, oh, which, was Brother putting on?
    That was something, it seemed, you just had to know.
But nobody knew, all afternoon,
    Though we studied and studied, as hard as we could, to know,

Studying the arithmetic of losses,
    To be prepared when the next one,
By fire, flood, foe, cancer, thrombosis,
    Or Time's slow malediction, came to be undone.

We studied all afternoon, till getting on to sun.
There was another lesson, but we were too young to take up that one.

VII Summer Storm (Circa 1916), and God's Grace

Toward sun, the sun flared suddenly red.
　　The green of woods was doused to black.
　　The cattle bellowed by the haystack.
Redder than ever, red clay was red.
　　Up the lane the plowhands came pelting back.

Astride and no saddle, and they didn't care
　　If a razor-back mule at a break-tooth trot
　　Was not the best comfort a man ever got,
But came huddling on, with jangling gear,
　　And the hat that jounced off stayed off, like as not.

In that strange light all distance died.
　　You know the world's intensity.
　　Field-far, you can read the aphid's eye.
The mole, in his sod, can no more hide,
　　And weeps beneath the naked sky.

Past silence, sound insinuates
　　Past ear into the inner brain.
　　The toad's asthmatic breath is pain,

The cutworm's tooth grinds and grates,
   And the root, in earth, screams, screams again,

But no cloud yet. No wind, though you,
   A half a county off, now spy
   The crow that, laboring zenith-high,
Is suddenly, with wings askew,
   Snatched, and tumbled down the sky.

And so you waited. You couldn't talk.
   The creek-side willows shuddered gray.
   The oak leaf turned the other way,
Gray as fish-belly. Then, with a squawk,
   The henhouse heaved, and flew away,

And darkness rode in on the wind.
   The pitchfork lightning tossed the trees,
   And God got down on hands and knees
To peer and cackle and commend
   His own sadistic idiocies.

Next morning you stood where the bridge had washed out.
   A drowned cow bobbled down the creek.
   Raw-eyed, men watched. They did not speak.
Till one shrugged, said he thought he'd make out.
   Then turned, took the woods-path up the creek.

Oh, send them summer, one summer just right,
   With rain well spaced, no wind or hail.
   Let cutworm tooth falter, locust jaw fail,
And if a man wake at roof-roar at night,
   Let that roar be the roar of God's awful Grace, and not of His flail.

VIII Founding Fathers, Nineteenth-Century Style, Southeast U.S.A.

They were human, they suffered, wore long black coat and gold watch chain.
They stare from daguerreotype with severe reprehension,
Or from genuine oil, and you'd never guess any pain
In those merciless eyes that now remark our own time's sad declension.

Some composed declarations, remembering Jefferson's language.
Knew pose of the patriot, left hand in crook of the spine or
With finger to table, while right invokes the Lord's just rage.
There was always a grandpa, or cousin at least, who had been, of course, a real Signer.

Some were given to study, read Greek in the forest, and these
Longed for an epic to do their own deeds right honor:
Were Nestor by pigpen, in some tavern brawl played Achilles.
In the ring of Sam Houston they found, when he died, one word engraved: *Honor.*

Their children were broadcast, like millet seed flung in a wind-flare.
Wives died, were dropped like old shirts in some corner of country.
Said, "Mister," in bed, the child-bride; hadn't known what to find there;
Wept all the next morning for shame; took pleasure in silk; wore the keys to the pantry.

39

"Will die in these ditches if need be," wrote Bowie, at the Alamo.
And did, he whose left foot, soft-catting, came forward, and breath hissed:
Head back, gray eyes narrow, thumb flat along knife-blade, blade low.
"Great gentleman," said Henry Clay, "and a patriot." Portrait by Benjamin West.

Or take those, the nameless, of whom no portraits remain,
No locket or seal ring, though somewhere, broken and rusted,
In attic or earth, the long Decherd, stock rotten, has lain;
Or the mold-yellow Bible, God's Word, in which, in their strength, they had also trusted.

Some wrestled the angel, and took a fall by the corncrib.
Fought the brute, stomp-and-gouge, but knew they were doomed in that glory.
All night, in sweat, groaned; fell at last with spit red and a cracked rib.
How sweet were the tears! Thus gentled they roved the dark land with their old story.

Some prospered, had black men and lands, and silver on table,
But remembered the owl call, the smell of burnt bear fat on dusk-air.
Loved family and friends, and stood it as long as able,
"But money and women, too much in ruination, am Arkansas-bound." So went there.

One of mine was a land shark, or so the book with scant praise
Denominates him, "a man large and shapeless,
Like a sack of potatoes set on a saddle," and says,
"Little learning but shrewd, not well trusted." Rides thus out of history,
                                             neck fat and napeless.

One saw Shiloh and such, got cranky, would fiddle all night.
The boys nagged for Texas. "God damn it, there's nothing, God damn it,
In Texas," but took wagons, went, and to prove he was right,
Stayed a year and a day, "hell, nothing in Texas," had proved it,
                                             came back to black vomit,

And died, and they died, and are dead, and now their voices
Come thin, like last cricket in frost-dark, in grass lost,
With nothing to tell us for our complexity of choices,
But beg us only one word to justify their own old life-cost.

40

So let us bend ear to them in this hour of lateness,
And what they are trying to say, try to understand,
And try to forgive them their defects, even their greatness,
For we are their children in the light of humanness, and under the shadow
of God's closing hand.

I X Foreign Shore, Old Woman, Slaughter of Octopus

What now do the waves say
   To her, the old woman? She wears peasant black,
Alone on the beach, barefoot, and the day
   Withdraws, and she follows her slow track
Among volcanic black boulders, at sea-edge, and does not look back.
Sea-tongue softly utters among boulders by her track.

Saffron-saddening the mountain, the sun
   Sinks, and from sea, black boulder by boulder,
Night creeps. She stops by the boulders, leans on one,
   And if from black shawl she should unfold her
Old hand to the stone, she would find it yet warm, but it will be colder.
What has soft sea-tongue among black boulders told her?

All day there was picnic and laughter,
   Bright eye and hair tossing, white foam and thigh-flash,
And up from some cold coign and dark lair of water,
   Ectoplasmic, snot-gray, the obscene of the life-wish,
Sad tentacles weaving like prayer, eyes wide to glare-horror of day-wash,
The nightmare was spread out on stone. Boys yelled at the knife flash.

The mountain is black, the sun drops.
   Among the black boulders, slow foam laces white.
Wind stirs, stirs paper of picnic, stops,
   And agleam in imperial ease, at sky-height,
One gull hangs white in contempt of our human heart, and the night.
Pearl-slime of the slaughter, on black stone, glints in last light.

What can the sea tell her,
   That she does not now know, and know how to bear?
She knows, as the sea, that what came will recur,
   And detached in that wisdom, is aware
How grain by slow grain, last sun heat from sand is expended on night air.
Bare flesh of old foot knows that much, as she stands there.

This is not my country, or tongue,
   And my age not the old woman's age, or sea-age.
I shall go on my errand, and that before long,
   And leave much but not, sea-darkling, her image,
Which in the day traffic, or as I stand in night dark, may assuage
The mind's pain of logic somewhat, or the heart's rage.

43

X Dark Night of

Far off, two fields away,
Where dark of the river-woods lay,
I saw him divulged into daylight,
And stand as to look left and right.
You could guess that quick look aside
Like a creature that knows how to hide
And does not debate pride.

Yes, the owner might come riding
With pistol in pocket, or striding
Along with a stout stick in hand,
To say: "Get the hell off my land!"
And the fellow would understand.

The owner would be justified
To clean him out, hoof-and-hide.
He might set your woods on fire,
Or at least mash down barbed wire.
That's all the excuse you require.

44

I was twelve, and my property sense
Was defective, though much improved since.
The day, anyway, was a scorcher,
So I didn't get up from the porch or
Even whistle the dogs from the shade
To provoke that flap-jawing parade
Of brute holler and whoop through the heat
To set a tooth in tramp-meat.
Didn't lay down my book, or even shout
Back into the house what was out,
How hedge-skulker and creature of night
And son of pellagra and spite
Now stood in our honest daylight.

Now stood, then slowly moved
One step. Stopped to see if he'd proved
That a man could survive half a minute
Outside the woods and not in it.
Looked back once to black safety of shade,
Then was caught in that great suction made
By the world's bright vacancy.
Was drawn by the world's blank eye.
Moved under the light-dizzy sky.

Far off, he is pin-prick size,
A mote dark in your dazzle of eyes.
He moves without truth or dimension
Across that vast space men should shun.
Lost and faceless and far,
Under light's malevolent stare,
In a painful retardation,
He moves toward what destination,
And so passes over
The enormity of clover.
Is now gone. Has passed over.

Now afternoon, strand by gold strand,
Raveled out, and over the land
Light leveled toward time set
For me to get up and forget
Egypt's arrogant dead
Or that Scaevola whom Rome bred.
Yes, time to drop book, and rouse,
And up and leave the house,
And round up the cows.

The cows drift up the lane.
White elder blooms by the lane.
They move in a motion like sleep.
Their jaws make a motion like sleep.
I linger, leaf by leaf.
Dust, pale, powders elder leaf,
And the evening-idle, pale sky
Drains your body light, and dry.
Air moves sweet through pale husk under sky.

But suddenly you are you,
No pale husk the air moves through.
My heart clenched hand-hard as I stood.
The adrenalin tingled my blood.
My lungs made a fish-gasp for air.
Cold prickles ran in my hair.
Beneath elder bloom, the eyes glare.

Couched under elder bloom,
In the honeysuckle he'd made room,
And the white strands regally wreathed
His old head, and the air he breathed
Was heavy with the languishment
Of that too sweet scent.
He was old, rough-grizzled, and spent.

Old and spent, but heaves up his head,
And our eyes thread the single thread
Of the human entrapment, until,
In a voice like a croak from an old well,
He says: "Caint you git on away?"
But I simply can't move away.
He says: "Caint you let a man lay!"

I stared down the dank depth and heard
That croak from cold slime. Then he stirred,
Jerked up, stumbled up in his lair,
Like an old mule snagged on barbed wire.
Jerked free, a moment stood there.

A little I stood there alone
To stare down the lane where he'd gone.
Then I turned to follow the cows
Up yonder toward the house,
There to enter and understand
My plate laid by a loving hand,
And to sleep, but not understand
That somewhere on the dark land,
Unable to stop or stand,
On a track no man would have planned,
By age, rage, rejection unmanned,
A bundle of rags in one hand,
Old black felt hat in other hand,
At last he would understand,
And with his old head bare
Move in the dark air.
His head, in the dark air,
Gleams with the absolute and glacial purity of despair.
His head, unbared, moves with the unremitting glory of stars high
in the night heaven there.
He moves in joy past contumely of stars or insolent indifference of the dark air.
May we all at last enter into that awfulness of joy he has found there.

XI Infant Boy at Midcentury

1 *When the Century Dragged*

When the century dragged, like a great wheel stuck at dead center;
When the wind that had hurled us our half-century sagged now,
And only velleity of air somewhat snidely nagged now,
With no certain commitment to compass, or quarter: you chose to enter.

You enter an age when the neurotic clock-tick
Of midnight competes with the heart's pulsed assurance of power.
You have entered our world at scarcely its finest hour,
And smile now life's gold Apollonian smile at a sick dialectic.

You enter at the hour when the dog returns to his vomit,
And fear's moonflower spreads, white as girl-thigh, in dusk of compromise;
When posing for pictures, arms linked, the same smile in their eyes,
Good and Evil, to iron out all differences, stage their meeting at summit.

You come in the year when promises are broken,
And petal fears the late, as fruit the early frost-fall;
When the young expect little, and old endure total recall,
But discover no logic to justify what they had taken, or forsaken.

48

But to take and forsake now you're here, and the heart will compress
Like stone when we see that rosy heel learn,
With its first step, the apocalyptic power to spurn
Us, and our works and days, and onward, prevailing, pass

To pause, in high pride of undisillusioned manhood,
At the gap that gives on the new century, and land,
And with calm heart and level eye command
That dawning perspective and possibility of human good.

2 Modification of Landscape

There will, indeed, be modification of landscape,
And in margin of natural disaster, substantial reduction.
There will be refinement of principle, and purified action,
And expansion, we trust, of the human heart-hope, and hand-scope.

But is it a meanness of spirit and indulgence of spite
To suggest that your fair time, and friends, will mirror our own
Somewhat, and ourselves, for flesh will yet grieve on the bone,
And the heart need compensation for its failure to study delight?

Some will take up religion, some discover the virtue of money.
Some will find liberal causes the mask for psychic disturbance.
Some will expiate ego with excessive kindness to servants,
And some make a cult of honor, having often quite little, if any.

Some, hating all humans, will cultivate love for cats,
And some from self-hate will give children a morbid devotion.
Some will glorify friendship, but watch for the slightest motion
Of eyelid, or lip-twitch, and the longed-for betrayal it indicates.

50

Success for the great will be heart-bread, and soul's only ease.
For some it will stink, like mackerel shining in moonlight.
At the mere thought of failure some will wet their sheets in the night,
Though some wear it proud as Kiwanis, or manhood's first social disease.

Yes, the new age will need the old lies, as our own once did;
For death is ten thousand nights—sure, it's only the process
Of accommodating flesh to idea, but there's natural distress
In learning to face Truth's glare-glory, from which our eyes are long hid.

3 *Brightness of Distance*

You will read the official histories—true, no doubt.
Barring total disaster, the record will speak from the shelf.
And if there's disaster, disaster will speak for itself.
So all of our lies will be truth, and the truth vindictively out.

Remember our defects, we give them to you gratis.
But remember that ours is not the worst of times.
We stand convicted of follies rather than crimes—
Yes, we throw out baby with bath, drop the meat in the fire where the fat is.

And in even such stew and stink as Tacitus
Once wrote of, his generals, gourmets, pimps, poltroons,
He found persons of private virtue, the old-fashioned stout ones
Who would bow the head to no blast; and we know that such are yet with us.

He puzzled how virtue finds perch past confusion and wrath;
How even Praetorian brutes, blank of love, as of hate,
Proud in their craftsman's pride only, held a last gate,
And died, and each back unmarred as though at the barracks bath.

52

And remember that many among us wish you well;
And once, on a strange shore, an old man, toothless and through,
Groped hand from the lattice of personal disaster to touch you.
He sat on the sand for an hour; said *ciao, bello,* as evening fell.

And think, as you move past our age that grudges and grieves,
How eyes, purged of envy, will follow your sunlit chance.
Eyes will brighten to follow your brightness and dwindle of distance.
From privacy of fate, eyes will follow, as though from the shadow of leaves.

XII Lullaby: Smile in Sleep

Sleep, my son, and smile in sleep.
You will dream the world anew.
Watching you now sleep,
I feel the world's depleted force renew,
Feel the nerve expand and knit,
Feel a rustle in the blood,
Feel wink or warmth and stir of spirit,
As though season woke in the heart's cold underwood.
The vernal work is now begun.
Sleep, my son.
Sleep, son.

You will see the nestling fall.
Blood flecks grass of the rabbit form.
You will, of course, see all
The world's brute ox-heel wrong, and shrewd hand-harm.
Throats are soft to invite the blade.
Truth invites the journalist's lie.
Love bestowed mourns trust betrayed,
But the heart most mourns its own infidelity.
The greater, then, your obligation.

Dream perfection.
Dream, son.

When the diver leaves the board
To hang at gleam-height in his sky,
Trajectory is toward
An image hung perfect as light in the mind's wide eye.
So your dream will later serve you.
So now, dreaming, you serve me,
And give our hope new patent to
Enfranchise the human possibility.
Grace undreamed is grace forgone.
Dream grace, son.
Sleep on.

Dream that sleep is a sunlit meadow
Drowsy with a dream of bees
Threading sun, and the shadow
Where you lie lulled by their sunlit industries.
Let the murmurous bees of sleep
Tread down honey in honeycomb.
Heart-deep now, your dream will keep
Sweet in that deep comb for time to come.
Dream the sweetness coming on.
Dream, sweet son.
Sleep on.

What if angry vectors veer
Around your sleeping head, and form?
There's never need to fear
Violence of the poor world's abstract storm.
For you now dream Reality.
Matter groans to touch your hand.
Matter now lifts like the sea
Toward that cold moon that is your dream's command.
Dream the power coming on.
Dream, strong son.
Sleep on.

XIII Man in Moonlight

1 Moonlight Observed from Ruined Fortress

Great moon, white-westering past our battlement,
Dark sea offers silver scintillance to your sky,
And not less responsive would my human heart be if I
Were duly instructed in what such splendors have meant.

I have thought on the question by other sea, other shore:
When you smoothed the sweet Gulf asleep, like a babe at the breast,
When the moon-lashed old freighter banged stars in Atlantic unrest,
When you spangled spume-tangle on black rock, and seal barked at sea-roar.

Décor must be right, of course, for your massive effect,
But a Tennessee stock-pond is not beneath your contempt,
Though its littoral merely a barnyard with cow-pats unkempt.
No, even a puddle is not too small for respect,

And once on the Cumberland's bluffs I stood at midnight,
With music and laughter behind me, while my eyes
Were trapped in gleam-glory, but the heart's hungry surmise
Faded; so back to the racket and bottle's delight.

56

Be it sea or a sewer, we know you have never much cared
What sort of excuse, just so you may preen and prink,
With vulgarities to make Belasco blink
And tricks that poor Houdini wouldn't have dared.

So now with that old, anguishing virtuosity
You strike our cliff, and then lean on to Carthage.
We stand on the crumbling stone and ruins of rage,
To watch your Tyrrhenian silver prank the sea.

And thus we enact again the compulsive story,
Knowing the end, the end, and ah, how soon,
But caught in strict protocol of plenilune
And that werewolf thirst to drink the blood of glory.

We stare, we stare, but will not stare for long.
You will not tell us what we need to know.
Our feet soon go the way that they must go,
In diurnal dust and heat, and right and wrong.

2   *Walk by Moonlight in Small Town*

Through the western window full fell moonlight.
It must have waked me where I lay.
Room objects swam in that spooky day.
I rose, dressed, walked the summer night,
As long years back I had moved in that compulsive light.

Lawns green by day now shimmered like frost.
Shadow, beast-black, in porches lurked.
On house fronts, windowpanes moon-smirked.
Past supper, paper read, lawn hosed,
How white, in the depth of dark rooms now, faces reposed.

Down Main Street, the window dummies blessed,
With lifted hand and empty stare,
The glimmering emptiness of air,
As though lunatically to attest
What hope the daylight heart might reasonably have possessed.

Three boxcars slept, as quiet as cows.
They were so tired, they'd been so far.
SP and *Katy, L & N R R —*

58

After bumble and bang, and where God knows,
They'd cracked the rust of a weed-rank spur, for this pale repose.

How long ago, at night, up that track,
I had watched the Pullmans flash and fade,
Then heard, in new quiet, the beat my heart made.
But every ticket's round-trip; now back,
I stood and again watched night-distance flee up that empty track.

I crossed the track, walked up the rise.
The school building hulked, ugly as day.
Beyond, the night fields fell away.
Building and grounds had shrunk in size,
And that predictable fact seemed pitiful to my eyes.

And pitiful was the moon-bare ground.
Dead grass, the gravel, earth ruined and raw—
It had not changed. And then I saw
That children were playing, with no sound.
They ceased their play, then quiet as moonlight, drew, slow, around.

Their eyes were fixed on me, and I
Now tried, face by pale face, to find
The names that haunted in my mind.
Each small, upgazing face would lie
Sweet as a puddle, and silver-calm, to the night sky.

But something grew in their pale stare:
Not reprobation or surprise,
Nor even forgiveness in their eyes,
But a humble question dawning there,
From face to face, like beseechment dawning on empty air.

Might a man but know his Truth, and might
He live so that life, by moon or sun,
In dusk or dawn, would be all one,
Then never on a summer night
Need he stand and shake in that cold blaze of Platonic light.

59

3   *Lullaby: Moonlight Lingers*

Moonlight lingers down the air.
Moonlight marks the window-square
As I stand and watch you sleep.
I hear the rustle where
The sea stirs sweet and sighs in its silvered sleep.
My son, sleep deep.
Sleep deep, son, and dream how moonlight
Unremitting, whitely, whitely, unpetals down the night.
As you sleep, now moonlight
Mollifies the mountain's rigor,
Laves the olive leaf to silver,
And black on moon-pale trunk of the olive
Prints shadow of the olive leaf.
Sleep, let moonlight give
Dark secondary definition to the olive leaf.
Sleep, son, past grief.

I might now close my eyes and see
Moonlight white on a certain tree.
It was a big white oak near a door

Familiar, long back, to me,
But now years unseen, and my foot enters there no more.
My son, sleep deep.
Sleep deep, son, and let me think
How moonlight glimmered down a summer lane to the cedar woods' dark brink.
Sleep, and let me now think
Of moon-frost white on black bough of cedar,
White moon-rinse on meadow, whiter than clover,
And at moon-dark stone, how water woke
In a wink of glory, slid on to sleep.
Sleep, let this moon provoke
Moonlight more white on that landscape lost in the heart's homely deep.
Son, past grief, sleep.

Moonlight falls on sleeping faces.
It fell in far times and other places.
Moonlight falls on your face now,
And now in memory's stasis
I see moonlight mend an old man's Time-crossed brow.
My son, sleep deep,
Though moonlight will not stay.
Moon moves to seek that empty pillow, a hemisphere away.
Here, then, you will wake to the day.
Those who died, died long ago,
Faces you will never know,
Voices you will never hear—
Though your father heard them in the night,
And yet, sometimes, I can hear
That utterance as if tongue-rustle of pale tide in moonlight:
Sleep, son. Good night.

XIV Mad Young Aristocrat on Beach

He sits in blue trunks on the sand, and children sing.
Their voices are crystal and sad, and tinkle in sunlight.
Their voices are crystal, and the tinkling
Of sadness, like gold ants, crawls on his quivering heart in its midnight.
And the sea won't be still, won't be still,
In that freaking and fracture and dazzle of light.
Yes, somebody ought to take steps and stop it.
It's high time that somebody did, and he thinks that he will.
Why, it's simple, it's simple, just get a big mop and mop it,
Till it's dry as a bone—you sea, you *cretino*, be still!
But he's tired, he is tired, and wants only sleep.
Oh, Lord, let us pray that the children stop singing before he begins to weep.

If he wept, we just couldn't bear it, but look, he is smiling!
He ponders how charming it is to smile, and magnanimous.
And his smile, indeed, is both sweet and beguiling,
And jóy floods his heart now like hope, to replace that old dark animus.
So look! at the great concert grand,
He is bowing, and bowing, and smiling now on us,
And smiles at the sea, at the sea's bright applause—

62

But fame, ah, how sad! Again he sits on the sand,
And thinks how all human rewards are but gauds and gewgaws,
And lets sand, grain by grain, like history slip from his hand.
But his mother once said that his smile was sweet.
Curse the bitch, it is power man wants, and like a black cloud now he mounts to his feet.

He is young and sun-brown and tall and well formed, and he knows it.
He will swim in the sea, the water will break to his will.
Now emerging on shore, he is lethal, he shows it.
Yes, let them beware that brute jaw-jut and eye cold now and still.
Yes, let him beware, beware,
That brother, the elder, who comes to the title.
But a title, *merde*! he will marry a passport,
And dollars, of course—he has blood, though he isn't the heir.
Then sudden as death, a thought stops him chillingly short:
Mais l'Amérique, merde! why it's full of Americans there.
So closes his eyes, longs for home, longs for bed.
Ah, that sweet-haunched new housemaid! But knows he can't get her except
                                        in the dark of his head.

So thinks of a whore he once had: she was dull as a sow,
And not once, never once, showed affection. He thinks he will cry.
Then thinks, with heart sweet, he'll be dead soon now,
And opens his eyes to the blaze and enormousness of the sky.
And we watch him, we watch him, and we
Are lonely, are lonely as death, though we try
To love him, but can't, for we sit on the sand,
Eyes throbbing at merciless brilliance and bicker of sea,
While sand, grain by grain, like our history, slips from his hand.
We should love him, because his flesh suffers for you and for me,
As our own flesh should suffer for him, and for all
Who will never come to the title, and be loved for themselves, at innocent nightfall.

X V Dragon Country: To Jacob Boehme

This is the dragon's country, and these his own streams.
The slime on the railroad rails is where he has crossed the track.
On a frosty morning, that field mist is where his great turd steams,
And there are those who have gone forth and not come back.

I was only a boy when Jack Simms reported the first depredation,
What something had done to his hog pen. They called him a God-damn liar.
Then said it must be a bear, after some had viewed the location,
With fence rails, like matchwood, splintered, and earth a bloody mire.

But no bear had been seen in the county in fifty years, they knew.
It was something to say, merely that, for people compelled to explain
What, standing in natural daylight, they agreed couldn't be true;
And saying the words, a man felt, in the chest, a constrictive pain.

At least, some admitted this later, when things had got to the worst,
When, for instance, they found, in the woods, the wagon turned on its side,
Mules torn from trace chains, and you saw how the harness had burst.
Spectators averted the face from the spot where the teamster had died.

64

But that was long back, in my youth, just the first of case after case.
The great hunts fizzled. You followed the track of disrepair,
Ruined fence, blood-smear, brush broken, but came, in the end, to a place
With weed unbent, leaf calm, and nothing, nothing, was there.

So what, in God's name, could men think, when they couldn't bring to bay
That belly-dragging earth-evil, but found that it took to air?
Thirty-thirty or buckshot might fail, but then at least you could say
You had faced it—assuming, of course, that you had survived the affair.

We were promised troops, the Guard, but the Governor's skin got thin
When up in New York the papers called him Saint George of Kentucky.
Yes, even the Louisville reporters who came to Todd County would grin.
Reporters, though rarely, still come. No one talks. They think it unlucky.

Things happen, but they are denied, as when on the road to go out
To the old Pinch 'Em Church, a salesman, traveling for Swift, or Armour,
Stepped from his car. The Sheriff said, accident caused by a blowout.
They burned up the car to explain lack of patronage for the embalmer.

If a man disappears—well, the fact is something to hide.
The family says, gone to Akron, or up to Ford, in Detroit.
When we found Jebb Johnson's boot, with the leg, what was left, inside,
His mother said, no, it's not his. So we took it out to destroy it.

Land values are falling, no longer do lovers in moonlight go.
The rabbit, thoughtless of air gun, in the nearest pasture cavorts.
Now certain fields go untended, the local birth rate goes low.
The coon dips his little black paw in the riffle where he nightly resorts.

Yes, other sections have problems somewhat different from ours.
Their crops may fail, bank rates rise, on rumor of war loans be called,
But we feel removed from maneuvers of Russia, or other great powers,
And from much ordinary hope are now disenthralled.

The Catholics have sent in a mission, Baptists report new attendance.
But that's not the point. We are human, and the human heart

Demands language for reality that has no slightest dependence
On desire, or need. Now in church they pray only that evil depart.

But if the Beast were withdrawn now, life might dwindle again
To the ennui, the pleasure, and night sweat, known in the time before
Necessity of truth had trodden the land, and heart, to pain,
And left, in darkness, the fearful glimmer of joy, like a spoor.

XVI Ballad of a Sweet Dream of Peace

1 *And Don't Forget Your Corset Cover, Either*

And why, in God's name, is that elegant bureau
Standing out here in the woods and dark?
Because, in God's name, it would create a furor
If such a Victorian piece were left in the middle of Central Park,
To corrupt the morals of young and old
With its marble top and drawer pulls gilt gold
And rosewood elaborately scrolled,
And would you, in truth, want your own young sister to see it in the Park?
But she knows all about it, her mother has told her,
And besides, these days, she is getting much older,
And why, in God's name, is that bureau left in the woods?
All right, I'll tell you why.
It has as much right there as you or I,
For the woods are God's temple, and even a bureau has moods.
But why, in God's name, is that elegant bureau left all alone in the woods?

It is left in the woods for the old lady's sake,
For there's privacy here for a household chore,
And Lord, I can't tell you the time it can take
To apply her own mixture of beeswax and newt-oil to bring out the gloss once more.

67

For the poor old hands move slower each night,
And can't manage to hold the cloth very tight,
And it's hard without proper light.
But why, in God's name, all this privacy for a simple household chore?
In God's name, sir! would you simply let
Folks see how naked old ladies can get?
Then let the old bitch buy some clothes like other folks do.
She once had some clothes, I am told,
But they're long since ruined by the damp and mold,
And the problem is deeper when bones let the wind blow through.
Besides it's not civil to call her a bitch, and her your own grandma, too.

2 Keepsakes

Oh, what brings her out in the dark and night?
She has mislaid something, just what she can't say,
But something to do with the bureau, all right.
Then why, in God's name, does she polish so much, and not look

in a drawer right away?
Every night, in God's name, she does look there,
But finds only a Book of Common Prayer,
A ribbon-tied lock of gold hair,
A bundle of letters, some contraceptives, and an orris-root sachet.
Well, what is the old fool hunting for?
Oh, nothing, oh, nothing that's in the top drawer,
For that's left by late owners who had their own grief to withstand,
And she tries to squinch and frown
As she peers at the Prayer Book upside down,
And the contraceptives are something she can't understand,
And oh, how bitter the tears she sheds, with some stranger's old letters in hand!

You're lying, you're lying, she can't shed a tear!
Not with eyeballs gone, and the tear ducts, too.
You are trapped in a vulgar error, I fear,

69

For asleep in the bottom drawer is a thing that may prove instructive to you:
Just an old-fashioned doll with a china head,
And a cloth body naked and violated
By a hole through which sawdust once bled,
But drop now by drop, on a summer night, from her heart it is treacle bleeds through.
In God's name, what!—Do I see her eyes move?
Of course, and she whispers, "I died for love,"
And your grandmother whines like a dog in the dark and shade,
For she's hunting somebody to give
Her the life they had promised her she would live,
And I shudder to think what a stink and stir will be made
When some summer night she opens the drawer and finds that poor self she'd mislaid.

3   Go It, Granny—Go It, Hog!

Out there in the dark, what's that horrible chomping?
Oh, nothing, just hogs that forage for mast,
And if you call, "Hoo-pig!" they'll squeal and come romping,
For they'll know from your voice you're the boy who slopped them

in dear, dead days long past.

Any hogs that I slopped are long years dead,
And eaten by somebody and evacuated,
So it's simply absurd, what you said.
You fool, poor fool, all Time is a dream, and we're all one Flesh, at last,
And the hogs know that, and that's why they wait,
Though tonight the old thing is a little bit late,
But they're mannered, these hogs, as they wait for her creaky old tread.
Polite, they will sit in a ring,
Till she finishes work, the poor old thing:
Then old bones get knocked down with a clatter to wake up the dead,
And it's simply absurd how loud she can scream with no shred of a tongue in her head.

71

4   *Friends of the Family, or Bowling a Sticky Cricket*

Who else, in God's name, comes out in these woods?
Old friends of the family, whom you never saw,
Like yon cranky old coot, who mumbles and broods,
With yachting cap, rusty frock coat, and a placard proclaiming, "I am the Law!"
What makes him go barefoot at night in God's dew?
In God's name, you idiot, so would you
If you'd suffered as he had to
When expelled from his club for the horrible hobby that taught him the nature of law.
They learned that he drowned his crickets in claret.
The club used cologne, and so couldn't bear it.
But they drown them in claret in Buckingham Palace!
Fool, law is inscrutable, so
Barefoot in dusk and dew he must go,
And at last each cries out in a dark stone-glimmering place,
"I have heard the voice in the dark, seeing not who utters. Show me Thy face!"

72

5   *You Never Knew Her Either, Though You Thought You Did, Inside Out*

Why now, in God's name, is her robe de nuit
So torn and bedraggled, and what is that stain?
It's only dried blood, in God's name, that you see.
But why does she carry that leaf in her hand? Will you try, in God's name, to explain?
It's a burdock leaf under which she once found
Two toads in coitu on the bare black ground,
So now she is nightly bound
To come forth to the woods to embrace a thorn tree, to try to understand pain,
And then wipes the blood on her silken hair,
And cries aloud, "Oh, we need not despair,
For I bleed, oh, I bleed, and God lives!" And the heart may stir
Like water beneath wind's tread
That wanders whither it is not said.
Oh, I almost forgot—will you please identify her?
She's the afternoon one who to your bed came, lip damp, the breath like myrrh.

73

6 *I Guess You Ought to Know Who You Are*

Could that be a babe crawling there in night's black?
Why, of course, in God's name, and birth-blind, but you'll see
How to that dead chestnut he'll crawl a straight track,
Then give the astonishing tongue of a hound with a coon treed up in a tree.
Well, who is the brat, and what's he up to?
He's the earlier one that they thought would be you,
And perhaps, after all, it was true,
For it's hard in these matters to tell sometimes. *But look, in God's name, I am me!*
If you are, there's the letter a hog has in charge,
With a gold coronet and your own name writ large,
And in French, most politely, "Répondez s'il vous plaît."
Now don't be alarmed we are late.
What's time to a hog? We'll just let them wait.
But for when you are ready, our clients usually say
That to shut the eyes tight and get down on the knees is the quickest and easiest way.

74

7   *Rumor Unverified Stop Can You Confirm Stop*

Yes, clients report it the tidiest way,
For the first time at least, when all is so strange
And helpers get awkward sometimes with delay.
But later, of course, you can try other methods that fancy suggests you arrange.
There are clients, in fact, who, when ennui gets great,
Will struggle, or ingeniously irritate
The helpers to acts I won't state:
For Reality's all, and to seek it, some welcome, at whatever cost, any change.
But speaking of change, there's a rumor astir
That the woods are sold, and the purchaser
Soon comes, and if credulity's not now abused,
Will, on this property, set
White foot-arch familiar to violet,
And heel that, smiting the stone, is not what is bruised,
And subdues to sweetness the pathside garbage, or thing body had refused.

XVII Boy's Will, Joyful Labor without Pay,
and Harvest Home (1918)

1 Morning

By breakfast time the bustle's on.
In the field the old red thresher clatters.
The old steam tractor shakes and batters.
Sweat pops already in the hot sun.
The dogs are barking, mad as hatters.

You bolt your oatmeal, up and go.
The world is panting, the world won't wait.
All energy's unregenerate.
Blood can't abide the status quo.
You run as far as the front gate,

Then stop. For when your hope is displayed
To wait you, you must feast the eye
An instant on possibility,
Before finite constriction is made
To our pathos of rapacity.

76

2 Work

The hand that aches for the pitchfork heft
Heaves sheaf from the shock's rich disrepair.
The wagoner snags it in mid-air,
Says, "Boy, save yore strength, 'fore you got none left,"
And grins, then wipes the sweat from his hair.

3   The Snake

Daylong, light, gold, leans on the land.
You stoke the tractor. You *gee* and *haw*.
You feed the thresher's gap-toothed maw.
Then on a load-top, high, you stand
And see your shadow, black as law,

Stretch far now on the gold stubble.
By now breath's short. Sweat stings the eyes.
Blue denim is sweat-black at the thighs.
If you make a joke, you waste your trouble.
In that silence the shout rings with surprise.

When you wreck a shock, the spot below
Is damp and green with a vernal gloom.
Field mouse or rabbit flees its doom,
And you scarcely notice how they go.
But a black snake rears big in his ruined room.

Defiant, tall in that blast of day,
Now eye for eye, he swaps his stare.

His outrage glitters on the air.
Men shout, ring around. He can't get away.
Yes, they are men, and a stone is there.

Against the wounded evening matched,
Snagged high on a pitchfork tine, he will make
Slow arabesque till the bullbats wake.
An old man, standing stooped, detached,
Spits once, says, "Hell, just another snake."

4 Hands Are Paid

The thresher now has stopped its racket.
It waits there small by the stack it has made.
The work is done, the hands are paid.
The silver dollar's in sweat-cold pocket,
And the shirt sticks cold to the shoulder blade.

Out of the field, the way it had come,
Dragging the thresher's list and bumble,
The tractor now, a-clank, a-shamble,
Grunts down the pike, the long way home.
In dusk, to water now, mules, slow, amble.

The dollar glints on the mantel shelf.
By the coal-oil lamp the man leans his head
Over fried sowbelly and cold corn bread.
He's too sleepy now to wash himself.
Kicks off his brogans. Gets to bed.

The bullbat has come, long back, and gone.
White now, the evening star hangs to preside

Over woods and dark water and far countryside.
The little blood that smeared the stone
Dropped in the stubble, has long since dried.

The springs of the bed creak now, and settle.
The overalls hang on the back of a chair
To stiffen, slow, as the sweat gets drier.
Far, under a cedar, the tractor's metal
Surrenders last heat to the night air.

In the cedar dark a white moth drifts.
The mule's head, at the barn-lot bar,
Droops sad and saurian under night's splendor.
In the star-pale field, the propped pitchfork lifts
Its burden, hung black, to the white star,

And the years go by like a breath, or eye-blink,
And all history lives in the head again,
And I shut my eyes and I see that scene,
And name each item, but cannot think
What, in their urgency, they must mean,

But know, even now, on this foreign shore,
In blaze of sun and the sea's stare,
A heart-stab blessed past joy or despair,
As I see, in the mind's dark, once more,
That field, pale, under starlit air.

81

XVIII Lullaby: A Motion like Sleep

Under the star and beech-shade braiding,
Past the willow's dim solicitudes,
Past hush of oak-dark and stone's star-glinted upbraiding,
Water moves, in a motion like sleep,
Along the dark edge of the woods.
So, son, now sleep.

Sleep, and feel how now, at woods-edge,
The water, wan, moves under starlight,
Before it finds that dark of its own deepest knowledge,
And will murmur, in motion like sleep,
In that leaf-dark languor of night.
So, son, sleep deep.

Sleep, and dream how deep and dreamless
The covered courses of blood are:
And blood, in a motion like sleep, moves, gleamless,
By alleys darkened deep now
In leafage of no star.
So, son, sleep now.

Sleep, for sleep and stream and blood-course
Are a motion with one name,
And all that flows finds end but in its own source,
And a circuit of motion like sleep,
And will go as once it came.
So, son, now sleep

Till clang of cock-crow, and dawn's rays,
Summon your heart and hand to deploy
Their energies and know, in excitement of day-blaze,
How like a wound, and deep,
Is Time's irremediable joy.
So, son, now sleep.

XIX The Necessity for Belief

The sun is red, and the sky does not scream.
The sun is red, and the sky does not scream.

There is much that is scarcely to be believed.

The moon is in the sky, and there is no weeping.
The moon is in the sky, and there is no weeping.

Much is told that is scarcely to be believed.

About the Author

Robert Penn Warren was born in Guthrie, Kentucky, in 1905. He entered Vanderbilt University at the age of sixteen to study for a scientific career, but found the study of literature more interesting. Having graduated *summa cum laude,* he went to the University of California for his master's degree, then to Yale University, and in 1928 to Oxford as a Rhodes scholar.

Upon returning to the United States, Mr. Warren turned to teaching—first at Southwestern College, then at Vanderbilt University. In 1934 he moved to Louisiana State University where, in addition to his teaching duties, he was one of the founders and editors of *The Southern Review,* one of our most distinguished literary magazines. From 1942 to 1950 he was Professor of English at the University of Minnesota, and in 1944–45 also served as Consultant in Poetry at the Library of Congress. From 1951 to 1956 he was a member of the faculty of Yale University.

Although he had already received a number of prizes for his poems, it was not until 1939 that Mr. Warren published his first novel, *Night Rider* (reissued by Random House in 1948), and won his first Guggenheim Fellowship. In 1943 came *At Heaven's Gate* and in 1946, *All the King's Men,* which won him the Pulitzer Prize. His fourth novel was *World Enough and Time* (Random House, 1950). *Brother to Dragons: A Tale in Verse and Voices,* appeared in 1953, and his most recent novel, *Band of Angels,* in 1955. Mr. Warren has also published three volumes of poetry and a short-story collection, *The Circus in the Attic,* in addition to many critical studies and textbooks.